May 4, 2006

To Cal + Lynn

Thank you for all your
support. Enjoy the Southwest
Experience! I so enjoyed
helping you with your Winter
Getaway! Blessings!

Linda DeWitt.

DESIGNER SHOWCASE

Interior Design at its Best

Melissa Cardona &
Nathaniel Wolfgang-
Price

Schiffer Publishing Ltd

4880 Lower Valley Road, Atglen, PA 19310 USA

Acknowledgments

Many thanks go to all the brilliant designers whose work is featured in this book, which wouldn't have been possible with their contribution of images, text, and editorial approval—kudos to you. Thanks also go to the many photographers whose gorgeous and captivating images appear in these pages. We appreciate your contribution. There were many others who played a major role in helping make this book a reality, and we thank you, too.

PHOTO CREDITS:
Cover photo courtesy of Sarah DeWitt, DeWitt Designs. Photography by Tim Fuller.

Photo on book's spine courtesy of James Rixner, Inc. Photography by Jay Rosenblatt.

Page 1 photo courtesy of Jon Jahr & Associates. Photography by Mark Lohman.

Page 2 photo courtesy of Susan Zises Green, Inc. Photography by Billy Cunningham.

Back cover photo courtesy of Joani Stewart, Montana Ave. Interiors. Photography by Douglas Hill.

Designed by "Sue"
Type set in Humanist 521 BT

ISBN: 0-7643-2398-9
Printed in China

Published by Schiffer Publishing Ltd.
4880 Lower Valley Road
Atglen, PA 19310
Phone: (610) 593-1777; Fax: (610) 593-2002
E-mail: Info@schifferbooks.com

For the largest selection of fine reference books on this and related subjects, please visit our web site at **www.schifferbooks.com**
We are always looking for people to write books on new and related subjects. If you have an idea for a book please contact us at the above address.

This book may be purchased from the publisher.
Include $3.95 for shipping.
Please try your bookstore first.
You may write for a free catalog.

In Europe, Schiffer books are distributed by
Bushwood Books
6 Marksbury Ave.
Kew Gardens
Surrey TW9 4JF England
Phone: 44 (0) 20 8392-8585; Fax: 44 (0) 20 8392-9876
E-mail: info@bushwoodbooks.co.uk
Free postage in the U.K., Europe; air mail at cost.

Simply Welcoming

Designer Mimi Love Guin wanted to keep the décor of this foyer as simple as possible, allowing the focus to remain on the space's stunning elliptical staircase and neo-classical architectural elements. Guin commissioned artist Charlotte Simpson-Baucom to paint a mural representing the rolling hills of the English Countryside above the curved moulded wood paneling. Glaze was painted over the mural to give it an antiqued and weathered look, adding a sense of history to the newly constructed home. Shiny Glass tile inlays in limestone flooring add interest, while maintaining a simple, elegant aesthetic. A French European inspired chandelier with graceful twists, curls, and turns, lit niches with urned moss balls, a grandfather clock, and a curved cane-back settee provide a perfectly balanced set of decorative elements to create a grand, and attractive, first impression.

Mimi Love Guin, Allied Member ASID,
    CQRID Certified, Interiors by
    Mimi, Inc.
2004 Homearama at Haeydon Hall—
    Charlotte, NC
Photography by Pat Shanklin

An Eloquent Welcome

Existing architecture and a large volume of space dictated the design of this foyer. Grand twin flying staircases, marble floors, Baccarret chandelier, and elegant arches and moldings offered a marvelous canvas from which designer Diane Replogle worked. The ceiling's warm spice color with gold leafing provided the starting point for the room's color palette, and was chosen for the room's four marbleized columns, which were finished using a 15th century Scagliola technique. Warm buttermilk colored walls, mulberry silk portiere at each pillar, and antique French furnishings, including an eighteenth century Louis XV piano and fauteuil chairs, finish off the space.

Diane Replogle, The Replogle House
    Interiors
2004 National Symphony Orchestra
    Decorators' Show House
Photography by Danielle Shankin

5

Grand Central Hall

With rooms radiating out from it like the spokes of a wheel, this grand, oval shaped hall acts as a hub of activity—functioning as dining room, den, and gallery. Designer Gail Green chose Art Moderne period styling to embellish the space, using a cubist-like painted wall motif, harlequin floor pattern, and modern materials. The use of hard and soft, light and dark, and cool and warm textures creates an exciting dynamic, perhaps best illustrated by the sconces with organic glass tops and geometric hammered bases.

Gail Green, Green & Company, Inc.
Ansonia Showhouse
Phillip Ennis Photography

Life's Passage

In this upstairs hall, designers Lori Graham and Lindsay Hair illustrate that a hallway should be more than simply a passage from room to room; it should capture that which is important to each of us: the people and places that define the uniqueness of our lives. Here, captivating black-and-white photographs by Renato Zacchia illustrate those aspects of life, giving form to those things that are beyond mere words. To balance the rich architectural detailing, the designers used simplicity to guide the way into a comfortably timeless aesthetic. The blue walls imbue a marine-like serenity, communicating tradition, quality, strength, and longevity: characteristics inherent to each of our life journeys.

Lori Graham Lindsay Hair Interiors
2004 National Symphony Orchestra
Decorators' Show House
Photography by Eric Johnson

Continental Cuisine

Designers from Pineapple House Interior Design took a modern approach to Continental design in this timeless and elegant kitchen. Accents in espresso, apple green, and china blue punctuate the room, where painted and glazed finishes and warm wood tones dominate. Modern furnishings, artwork, and accessories were used to update the traditional space. The butler's pantry echoes the refined mix of periods and styles with a contemporary painting juxtaposed above a finely detailed Louis XVI style demilume console. The creative milieu of styles, periods, colors, and textures crescendo in this sophisticated, inviting kitchen.

Pineapple House Interior Design®
2003 Atlanta Symphony Associates
    Decorators' Show House and
    Gardens
Photography by John Umberger, Real
    Images

Beaux Appétit

A kitchen design rooted in Beaux Arts architecture mixes classical sensibility with 21st century convenience and state of the art appliances. Limestone and rare marbles reminiscent of Pompeii ruins give the appearance of ancient reclaimed stone to backsplashes and flooring. Renaissance inspired bronze details and hand-forged tack add a jewel-like accent to the backsplash. Honed limestone countertops round out the rich selection of materials in warm color tones and textures.

Carolyn E. Oliver, Oliver's – A Design Studio
2003 Assistance League® of Southern California Design House
Peter Christiansen Valli Photographic Services

Work Kitchen

Kammy Kenman found inspiration for this kitchen in a well-known confectionery and lunch establishment in Los Angeles County. A tin ceiling, traditional style cabinets, and historically inspired textiles create a Victorian atmosphere that maintains a fresh, contemporary feel with the addition of stainless steel appliances. Glass ornaments hanging from the light fixture add sparkle to the sun-drenched space. Ornamentation combines with functionality to create a truly spectacular room.

Kammy Kenman, Crème Fresh For the
    Home
2003 Assistance League® of Southern
    California Design House
Charles S. White Photography

Kitchen in the Round

A classical kitchen exudes grace and permanence with its classically refined style. Combining antiqued white cabinetry and warm, walnut wood, designer Joyce Hoshall was able to create an impressive, yet inviting space. Details like the fresco-painted circular ceiling, grape carved corbels, and antique finishes imbue a historic quality, heightened by the use of cabinetry-costumed appliances. In the adjacent, open breakfast room, furniture-like hutches, a built-in bench, and a fireplace add coziness to grand styling.

Joyce Hoshall Interiors, Antiques, & Collections
2004 Eureka School District Foundation Home Show
Photography by Dave Adams

Textural Appeal

Susie Johnson wanted to create a serene kitchen with classic contemporary lines—a room that was sophisticated but still inviting. Stainless steel cabinetry hardware, copper pendants, Juperana Tabaca granite countertops, and a stainless steel bracket around the island establish a modern aesthetic, while the lines of the maple and cherry cabinets achieve the warmth the designer was looking for. Maple flooring and a matte-finished Portuguese Limestone backsplash with copper accent tiles add to the rich blend of natural textures complemented with stainless steel accents and appliances throughout.

Susie Johnson Interior Design, Inc.
2001 Austin Symphony Designer Show House
Photography by Mark Knight

The Chef's Kitchen

Carolyn E. Oliver pays homage to trend-setting Milan with this kitchen that serves up the best in historic and contemporary design, while respecting the home's Italian influenced architecture. Professional grade kitchen appliances along with warm, inviting, and clean lined styling create an ideal venue where chefs perform their craft with ease and flair.

Carolyn E. Oliver, Oliver's – A Design Studio
2005 Pasadena Showcase House of Design
Peter Christiansen Valli Photographic Services

Fitted Just Right

This show house kitchen and morning room design incorporates a fresh interpretation of the classical Victorian Kitchen. Clive Christian fitted furniture—which is crafted in England, then hand-painted on site—defines the look of the room. Raised and fielded panels, Belgravia mantle and hidden storage for spices, corbelled and reeded pilasters, beveled glazed dressers, fluted frieze, and dentil cornice, all in an elegant glazed classic cream color, are a testament to quality. Integrated appliances serve the needs of a modern, fast-paced lifestyle, while classical design shows attention to detail and an appreciation for the finer things in life.

Rosalia M. Kallivokas, Clive Christian
    Washington
2005 National Symphony Orchestra
    Decorators' Show House
Photography by Angie Seckinger

20

Bistro Style

With styling inspired by the friendly feeling of a New York Bistro, designers Robert Schwartz and Karen Williams put all of the best features of a professional kitchen into this residential space. Without being overly showy or ornate, they created a beautiful kitchen functional enough to be used by a casual or a serious cook. Marble tile walls reminiscent of the New York subway show through custom glass-fronted cabinets without backs. Floor tiles laid in an eye-catching mini brick bond pattern maintain the polished, urban feel. Behind the range, the original window was tiled over to hide an unsightly view. In order to counteract the loss of daylight, sconces were placed around the kitchen's perimeter, and an ornamental European antique crystal chandelier was hung from the tin ceiling. The end result is a room that is functional and beautiful in its simplicity.

Robert Schwartz and Karen Williams,
    St. Charles of New York
2003 Kips Bay Decorator Show House
Photography by Keith Scott Morton

Arts & Crafts Adaptation

Antiqued cabinetry and Venetian plaster walls with a glazed finish, custom copper hood with aged patina, limestone farmhouse sink, and authentic antique armoire set a traditional tone in this kitchen. Designer Jackie Naylor used a rich contrast of light colored surfaces and dark accents to create interest in this refurbished 1920s kitchen. In the breakfast area, lace-covered, glass-fronted cabinets replaced a wall of cabinetry, while the cultured stone fireplace was included to establish an inviting atmosphere.

Jackie Naylor Interiors, Inc.
2001 Judd Showhouse
Photography by Robert Thien Photography

Indoor *Al Fresco*

Neo-Classical style tented walls give the impression of dining in an outdoor pavilion. Designer Jon Jahr wanted to maintain a traditional aesthetic in this dining room, where Adam style architectural elements are complemented by Art Deco, Regency, Empire, and Georgian style furnishings and accessories. The masculine chandelier is softened by the tromp l'oeil ceiling, for the finishing touches on an elegantly sophisticated room.

Jon Jahr & Associates, Inc.
2004 Pasadena Showcase House of
    Design
Mark Lohman Photography

Elegant Entertaining in Signature Style

Designer Douglass Weiss created this room for a young and lively family with a style that is both elegant and light. With its sleek lines, the circular table provides contemporary contrast to the room's antiques. Refined silk damask draperies soften the large expanse of windows and create an interesting transition for the casual, tactile wall covering. The walls feature the designer's signature element: a unique backdrop with a grid pattern, this time using French blue grass cloth.

Douglas Weiss Interiors
2004 Alliance Children's Theater Guild
    Christmas House
Photography by Erica George Dines

Freshly French

This dining room recalls the graciousness of continental dining in French inspired décor. Elegant chandeliers shed soft light onto a custom designed Yew wood elliptical dining room table set with white Italian ceramic china. Providing the basis for the room's color palette, a 1920s French painting of Diana the Huntress gives an ethereal feeling to the room. A Manuel Canovas linen fabric with a large scale white floral pattern on a lime green background was used for the window treatments, as well as to upholster two host chairs for an effect that is stunning, rounding out the brilliance of a traditional style room made fresh with a contemporary approach to design.

Marilyn M. Poling, ASID, Interior
    Impressions, Inc.
2004 National Symphony Orchestra
    Decorators' Showhouse
Angie Seckinger Photography

Dining Today

Warm, glowing woods with rich red accents enhance a room designed for gathering the family together. The dining table, accented with an iron stretcher, is teamed up with chairs covered in a plush, patterned chenille. On the floor is a custom-made Gothic-inspired rug. A soft green ceiling adds overhead interest. Textured walls of taupe and soft camel, a whimsical, hand-blocked linen print for draperies, and shdes that fold up from the bottom create a pastiche appealing to the senses.

Cheryl Womack, IFDA, and Alison Womack, ASID, Cheryl Womack Interiors
2001 Atlanta Symphony Associates Decorators' Show House and Gardens
Schilling Photography

Serving Up Warmth

Suzanne Tyler Design & Chinese Red
2004 Children's Museum of Southeastern Connecticut Showhouse
Photography by William Grant

This turn of the century butler's pantry was updated to create a warm and welcoming, family-friendly space. Envisioning the room as the heart of the house, Suzanne Tyler imbued the room with warmth-giving details. The linoleum floors were replaced with peach toned limestone. The walls were painted in a vertical ombre pattern, beginning with a dark chili red fading subtly through oranges to yellow. The room's focal point and dominant feature is a built-in wall unit. Originally painted start white, the designer decided to repaint it with a faux bois finish. Mirrors were installed in the recessed panels in order to create some additional depth. An absolute black granite countertop and handmade copper sink add character and texture.

French Delight

According to designer Diane Burgoyne, "Dining rooms do not have to be formal and stuffy. In the French countryside, the dining room evokes a place of comfort where family and friends can gather to share a meal and enjoy one another's company." With that idea in mind the designer chose to decorate this room in a French Provençal style. The furnishings, curtains, rug, and fireplace tiles are all French or inspired by French design. The chairs are upholstered and designed to be comfortable for dinner guests who intend to stay at the table and talk long after the meal is over. A small table and a pair of armchairs offer an excellent place for friends to take tea or to sit and have a chat. Bold use of dramatic shades of red, yellow, and green help establish a comfortable feel and serve to brighten the room. The fireplace in this dining room is covered with hand-painted tiles characteristic of the French Provençal style. With its warm colors, rustic decorations, and comfortable furniture, this dining room is one step away from the French countryside that inspired it.

Diane Burgoyne, Allied Member ASID, IFDA, Diane Burgoyne Interiors
2001 Lourdes Health System Show House
Photography by Elizabeth Hill

Sea, Sky, Earth, & Wine: This is the Life

Designer Sarah DeWitt was presented with a dining room she described as "a giant white box." To add warmth and scale down the room's enormous dimensions, antique wood beams were placed over the ceiling that was painted a coral color and glazed to blend in with the wood. Two shades of blue-green custom colored plaster were used to create interest and add age to the walls. The dining room's furnishings represent a mix of antiques, reproductions, and handmade treasures. Couture window treatments trimmed in velvet gimp and beads in the form of diamond gussets echo the subtle use of a harlequin pattern found throughout the space, while the multicolored stripe adds fresh playfulness to what might otherwise be considered a formal space. A family tree mural and faux stone coat of arms represent the generations of family that have resided in the home, adding a cherished, personal touch.

Sarah DeWitt, DeWitt Designs
2005 Tucson Museum of Art Designer
    Showhouse
Photography by Tim Fuller and Robin
    Stancliff

Whimsy in the Dining Room

Upholstered walls set an exotic and whimsical tone in this show house dining room, where stylized monkeys frolic in vibrantly colored tropical foliage. Rather than the typical formal approach to dining room décor, designer Robert Couturier wanted the room to provide the casual atmosphere associated with the shore, establishing a style defined by tropical beach elegance. The oblong rectangular shape of the room provided a challenge to Couturier, one which he met with the exciting juxtaposition of furnishings and accessories in a variety of shapes, sizes, and styles.

Robert Couturier, Inc.
2005 The Hamptons Showhouse
Photography by Billy Cunningham

The Dining Room: A Study in Gold & Red

Red accents punctuate a dining room rich in textures, patterns, and a playful sensibility that softens the space's classical formality. Paneled walls feature a subtle harlequin motif in neutral tones and trim that draws the eyes upward. Alternating around the dining room table, distinctly upholstered chairs add interest in tandem with a leopard and rose patterned rug. Overall, the room's décor adds a lively dynamic to classic architectural elements and creates an unforgettable dining experience.

Pauline Vastardis Interiors
2004 Deborah Hospital Foundation
    Designers' Show House
Photography by Barry Halkin

Balancing Act

The dining room of a contemporary Frank Lloyd Wright-influenced house was a well traveled, transitional space that seemed off-balance due to five doors, two walls of windows, and a seven-foot cove ceiling around its perimeter. The designers included a three-piece bookshelf in order to turn the dining room into a multi-purpose space, while a custom oversized limestone top table was used to anchor the room's design. A mahogany buffet on one wall was balanced with a custom folding screen that also served to add intimacy by shielding a portion of the room's many windows and glass doors. Mohair host and hostess chairs, linen benches, and suede saddle stools were chosen to soften the room's appearance, as well as to add a supple touch of color. A stunning chandelier made from a rectangular steel pan supporting hollowed out and electrified wax pillar candles lends light, warmth, and romance to the room.

Pineapple House Interior Design®
2004 Atlanta Symphony Associates
    Decorators' Show House and
    Gardens
Emily Followill Photography

Haute Couture

Designers Tim and Linda Arbogast wanted to create a haut couture dining room, merging classic pieces with contemporary elements in a vivid and graphic union of old and new. Greco-roman busts placed on lacquered steel pedestals and gold leafed antlers mounted on clear Lucite contrast with black on black Gucci wallpaper and a Mid-Century white sideboard. An antique Waterford crystal chandelier hangs above a table draped with a taffeta tablecloth trimmed with black silk ribbon. On the table is the room's centerpiece, a Japanese maple tree in a gold-leaf bowl. A black and white zebra-striped rug complements the black and white furnishings and injects an energetic dynamic into the room. The final result is a room that is surprising and vivid in its colors and unique in its mix of modern and classical décor.

Tim & Linda Arbogast, Arbogast
    Design Group
2005 Junior League of Sacramento
    Showcase House
Photography by Tee Taylor

Wine Lounge

Kammy Kenman designed this space for a wine collector, providing ample storage for bottles and wine glasses, and a tasting lounge filled with the fragrance of wine. The lounge area features an Old World finish on the walls and wooden beams on the ceiling to give the space a sense of history. Intended for hosting formal wine tastings and informal gatherings with family and close friends, the furnishings in the lounge were chosen for both style and for comfort. A porcelain farmhouse sink allows hands and glasses to be washed. Like a good glass of wine, this room combines color and taste to produce an elegant experience.

Kammy Kenman, Crème Fresh for the Home

2004 Assistance League® of Southern California Design House

Charles S. White Photography

Villa Cellar

This temperature-controlled wine cellar consists of wine racks which hold about 800 bottles of wine. Display areas exhibit rare bottles and an iron and stone console on the wall acts as a counter to set down glasses and pour wine. The outer part of the room is the "tasting room" where guests enjoy trompe l'oeil scenery of vineyards through an arched window and the trickle of water from a tiled fountain on the wall. A custom designed arched mirror hangs on the wall opposite the "window" to reflect the same scene on both sides of the room. Wooden beams were added to enhance the effect of a Tuscan Villa. A hand-painted table was custom designed for the space and was assembled in the room due to the narrow vault door. Antique Italian chairs round out the ensemble, and provide an unforgettable, almost-authentic Italian wine country experience.

Joani Stewart, Montana Ave Interiors
2001 Assistance League® of Southern
    California Design House
Photography by Douglas Hill

Shakespeare in the Wine Cellar

This space includes design elements not often seen in a show house setting. Danish style is reflected by bleached flooring, walls, and wine racks contrasted by resplendent blues, copper, and bronze. Cozy charm (*'hyggelig'* in Danish) is created using old and new, sleek and soft, fun and profound. The working wine cellar includes basic racks enhanced by a hand-painted Scandinavian pattern. The racks and wine are brilliantly illuminated by a bronze rail system. Luxury vinyl plank flooring is presented as an alternative to ceramic tile and the cellar is warmly framed by a full-view door with delicate bronze hardware. The elegant elliptical WILLEM SMITH credenza, inspired by the art nouveau/deco era, holds the tasting fare and Royal Copenhagen china and stemware. A glowing copper mesh and bronze buffet lamp throws a flaming light upon the quote above, "This above all: to thine own self be true…" from Shakespeare's Hamlet. The mirror above the credenza reflects the Danish Prince. Upon an antique Persian Sarouk Farahan, two vintage mid-century German salon chairs surround the prince and the "Hamlet" table, designed for Howarth Designs by WILLEM SMITH. Soft light glows from a Poul Henningsen spun copper pendant, creating a perfect setting in which to sip wine and ponder Shakespeare's words.

Dolly Howarth, Howarth Designs LLC
2005 National Symphony Orchestra
   Decorators' Show House
Angie Seckinger Photography

Receiving Salon

This room is a modern interpretation of a 1920s Venetian fantasy, where designer James Rixner combines ethereal, cool colors with smooth textures to create a tranquil, elegant space. Luxurious finishes and couture craftsmanship combined with fine period pieces and a rare 1920s Aubusson Art Deco carpet result in over the top glamour. The custom sofa mirrors the curve of an adjacent railing and welcomes visitors with open arms. Upholstered walls abound with dressmaker details. The individually sewn, color coordinated silk diamonds are installed in a harlequin pattern and hand tufted with mother-of-pearl buttons. A 1940s Murano Chandelier reflects the room's dotted white and gold leaf ceiling treatment, while recessed framing projectors illuminate the vintage Venetian street scenes. This stunning space is truly a showstopper.

James Rixner, Inc.
2003 Kips Bay Decorator Show House
Photography by Jay Rosenblatt

Melodic by Design

From the delicious texture of the rug to the almost chartreuse mohair covering the bespoke sofa, this room is rich in texture and comfort. Silk, wool, and linen fabrics and elegant materials, including precious woods, bronze, and mica, convey a sense of quiet luxury...without excess. By design this space *feels* special: a perfect setting for listening to music or curling up with a great book. Simple, sumptuous, and warm—this room invites occupants to savor the music that is life.

James Hawes, Caldwell-Beebe Ltd.,
    Inc.
2003 National Symphony Orchestra
    Decorators' Show House
Photography by Gordon Beall

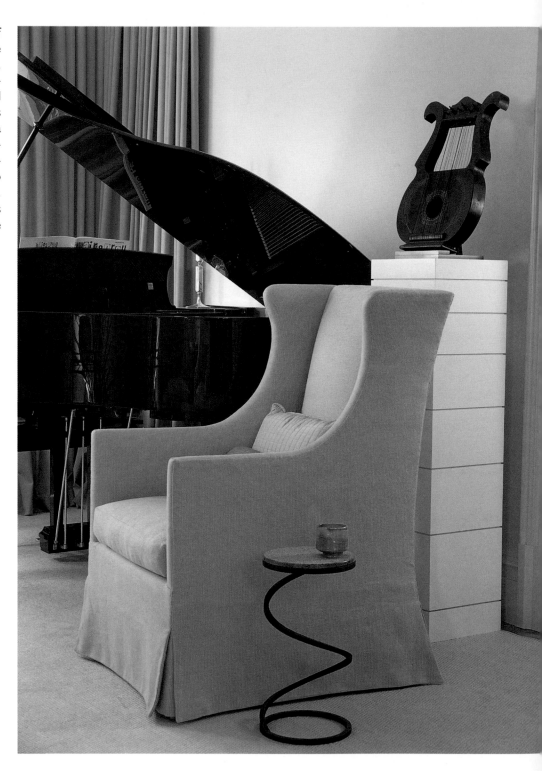

Her Retreat

This classic room for a woman in the entertainment field provides space for relaxing alone or entertaining friends and family. A custom designed mahogany wall unit with Art Deco molding and Roman X detailing anchors the room and holds state of the art electronics. A custom sofa covered in a tapestry Kravet fabric, cameo pink Spinneybeck leather ottoman, and Egyptian Mahal rug help to establish the room's mushroom and pale pink color palette, while contemporary paintings provide contrast. Venetian plaster walls were painted in an iridescent mushroom color and shine in the light from the television, Schoenbeck rock crystal chandelier, and Donghia Venetian glass lamps. Classic elements and modern styling create a vibrant atmosphere suitable for an entertainment diva.

Tere Bresin, ASID, Beret Design
    Group, Inc.
The 2004 Designer Showhouse of
    New Jersey
Photography by Daniel Eifert

The Lounge

Classic architectural elements and contemporary décor combine to create an energy-filled space that gives the sense of permanence. A set of black and white abstract prints on the wall serve to complement the black and white rug with a geometric pattern that seems to move from one end of the room to the other. Convex mirrors hung on the wall and a glass table were included to reflect light and add depth to the room, which is dominated by the dark wood walls. The long, white sofa also has a lightening effect.

John Barman, Inc.
2000 Kips Bay Decorator Show House
Photography by Billy Cunningham

A Family Gathering Room

For Susan Gulick Interiors, color is the heart of every home. In this Family Room, Susan used a rich array of textiles to present a tonal palette that flows from the stone of the fireplace and transforms the room. This nucleus of color is supported by rich glazed wood paneling, textural walls, and a hand-painted ceiling. The furnishings incorporate favorite antiques and a diverse sprinkling of eclectic touches. The room exudes a classically fresh and uncluttered personality. A retreat for soothing relaxation.

Susan Gulick Interiors
2004 National Symphony Orchestra
    Decorators' Show House
Photography by Judy Davis,
    Hoachlander Davis Photography

Subtle Contrast

Neutral tones of beige, off white and soft teal in a room with airy ceilings inspire a tranquil and serene atmosphere. Balance between old and new creates an invigorating dynamic where antiques soften the clean, crisp lines of contemporary furnishings; and an elegant chandelier shows traditional sensibility against a backdrop of contemporary sculptures and paintings. This room provides a relaxing venue for entertaining or quiet isolation.

Marilyn Poling, Interior Impressions, Inc.
2005 National Symphony Orchestra Decorators' Show House
Photography by Angie Seckinger

Avant-Garde Sitting Room

In this sitting room, James Rixner wanted to create a "Hamptons look without the usual beach clichés." By using modern pieces with a decidedly '60s look, he is recalling a time when the Hamptons was a haven for avant-garde artists. The room is carefully orchestrated in a symphony of green and blue hues that create a calming atmosphere. A perfectly scaled custom sectional in pale ginko silk with pillows and ottoman covered in an awning stripe velvet invite relaxing moments. The dramatic full height fireplace sheathed in luminous pale pistachio onyx is the perfect architectural statement. This serene and timeless room is a realization of Rixner's liveable, elegant aesthetic.

James Rixner, Inc.
2003 Hampton Designer Showhouse
Photography by Jay Rosenblatt

Lady's Retreat

Far from the noise and activity of a large household, this small room is the perfect place for the lady of the house to get away. A mix of subtle shades of beige and tan create a soothing atmosphere perfect for relaxing, while bright hints of red, orange, yellow, and pink add cheerfulness and vibrancy. An orange poppy photograph on canvas by Pip Bloomfield creates the color scheme for the room. A lacquered coffee table, linen-upholstered walls with a soft eucalyptus pattern, and silk pillows add dynamic texture to the room. Colors, textures, and décor come together in a harmonious whole ideal for rest, relaxation, and renewal.

Joani Stewart, Montana Ave Interiors
2004 Assistance League® of Southern
    California Design House
Photography by Peter Christiansen Valli

Now & Zen—A Room Where East Meets West

As an exercise in contemporary and Asian fusion, designers Victor js Liberatore, ASID, and Gail Lieberman exercised restraint and purity of form in their design for this sitting room. Two area rugs define the room's multiplicity and create two distinct seas of activity—with both game and relaxation areas framed by expanses of hand rubbed walls ushering the past into the future, with a built-up patina of red lacquer and ivory silk drapery and wall panels. As a striking graphic, the designers created two back-lit forms designed as geometric coolie's hats that grace the silk matlesse walls and set the mood aglow. A sunny window-side banquet, with light-filtering matchstick blinds affords additional seating for conversation or going solo with a good novel. Framing the banquet is a display niche housing Chinese generals, hand puppets, and oriental obelisk forms. The walls of the niche are decorated with hand-applied Asian newspaper clippings, adding another dimension to the details. The room's balance of sculptural and whimsical touches echoes an Asian and contemporary fusion…one that creates a wow factor.

Victor js Liberatore, ASID, Victor
    Liberatore Interior Design, and
    Gail Liberman
2004 Baltimore Symphony Orchestra
    Decorators' Show House
Alan Gilbert Photography

Gallery Landing

The walls of this warm, stylish room were faux painted to provide a background for a collection of original paintings. Warm colors provide a welcoming effect, and a camel silk mohair sofa is an invitation to sit and relax. A leopard print rug adds some excitement to the room and provides contrast to the sophisticated solids of the sofa and terra-cotta-hued silk window treatments, which feature chocolate-colored under panels. Accent lamps on either side of the sofa supplement the light coming in from the windows and a feathered pillow adds just a touch of whimsy.

Douglas Weiss Interiors
2002 Atlanta Symphony Associates
    Decorators' Show House and
    Gardens
Photography by Emily Followill

Terrace Salon

To complement the architecture and feel of the home, this living room was designed in a Parisian style using the principles of Feng Shui. The result was an elegant and comfortable space, ideal for entertaining. The neutral fabric on the sofa and armchairs was chosen to complement the limestone fireplace. Chocolate brown and celadon green were used throughout the room to provide contrast and warmth, while the beaded pillows on the sofa were chosen to add a glamorous twist to the space. A custom-designed folding mirrored screen adds balance and elegance to the room. The area's proximity to the windows makes it ideal for anyone who wants to sit down and relax with a good book. Glass doors let in light and can be opened to allow guests to mingle freely in the salon and out on the terrace.

Harmonious Living by Tish Mills Design Group, LLC
2005 Atlanta Symphony Associates Decorators' Show House and Gardens
Ken Rada Photography

Chocolate Luscious Living Room

Rich chocolate-colored walls surround this room with warmth and provide an excellent foundation for the rest of the features of the space. White trim and pillars accentuate the dark colors of the walls, while red punctuates the room with strong, vibrant color. Mirrors on top of the fireplace mantle draw the focus in the room and are complemented by silver and pewter ornaments throughout.

Joyce Hoshall Interiors, Antiques & Collections
2005 Junior League of Sacramento Designer Showcase House
Dave Adams Photography

Back to the Basics

A room rich in striking juxtapositions is marked by a hint of the home's original English Cottage style. A Zebra-stripe ottoman first catches the eye, which is then attracted to the complementary black-and-white abstract paintings. Raw textures and natural accents give the room a primal quality, while the custom light fixture recalls postmodernist design and the miniature bust adds classical accent. Industrial and natural, primitive and modern, physical and abstract, this room is one where the senses are stimulated and the mind is free to wander.

Joyce Hoshall Interiors, Antiques & Collections
2005 Sacramento Crisis Nursery Showhouse
Dave Adams Photography

Serene Library Retreat

Behind the doors of this room lurks a space dedicated to peace and quiet, a retreat from the hectic atmosphere of the house. Serving a dual function, a yin-yang shaped table can be set in the middle of the room as a coffee table or it can be pulled apart and used as a pair of end tables. Recessed bookshelves decorated with small, antiqued mirror keys house books suitable for browsing or for deeper contemplation. The interiors of the bookshelves are silver leafed and antiqued to match the mirrors. A refreshment bar features a limestone countertop and a sink with a basin made of onyx tiles set in a checkerboard pattern. A hand-blown glass light fixture adds an artful touch to the space. Walls in a soothing combination of gold and ivory Venetian plaster are stenciled, hand-painted, and stamped in gold. Central to the room is a fireplace. The surround is covered with small tumbled onyx tiles set in a herringbone pattern. Beneath the surround is a hearth made from limestone that was stained to match. Overall, this is a space that glows with light and a relaxing atmosphere.

Nancy Van Natta Associates
2004 Marin Designers Showcase
Photography by Alan Blaustein

A Reinterpretation of the Past

This living room combines the formality and elegance of classic European grand parlors with the more casual feel of a contemporary lifestyle. The use of luxurious silks, mohairs, and trims was inspired by the formal gathering rooms of the past, but were chosen in patterns reinterpreted for the twenty-first century.

Robin Muto, Positive Environments
    Interior Design Studio
2004 Rochester Philharmonic Orchestra Symphony Showhouse
Photography by *Design NY Magazine*

The Cigar Room

A gentleman's club-inspired room includes contemporary and traditional elements that are seamlessly married in an eclectic blend of furniture, art, and accessories. Tweed fabric upholstered walls and nail head trim set a masculine tone for the room, creating a club-like atmosphere enhanced by wall-mounted antlers. An operating humidor cabinet anchors the space, providing the perfect place for displaying a valued collection of cigars and cigar boxes. Lounge chairs placed in a diagonal orientation add interest, while an oversized area rug ties the seating circle together. Blue fabrics lighten the area, which maintains a club environment with the use of paisley slipcovers. Blue was also repeated in the ceiling, offering a sense of serenity. The Cigar Room is a calming refuge that refreshes and prepares one for enjoying and contemplating the many adventures life has to offer.

Corey McIntosh, McIntosh Interiors
2005 Atlanta Symphony Associates
    Decorators' Show House and
    Gardens
Photography by Ken Rada

Edwardian Sitting Room

A reproduction Bessarabian rug and the room's 1906 Colonial Revival architectural elements provided the inspiration for this Edwardian sitting room's design and color palette. Deep reds, sage greens, and golden straw colors are reflected throughout the room's fabrics, establishing a warm autumn atmosphere. The walls were treated with a Venetian plaster finish in Urban Putty color, which adds texture and depth in contrast to the silk and damask fabrics in the window treatments and furniture. A pair of contemporary oil paintings above the drinks cart keep the room feeling fresh, while 19th century engravings titled "Conchology" punctuate the seating area. Balance of design, colors, and textures unite this classic room, where friends gather for enjoyment.

Deborah Leamann Interiors
2001 Junior League of Greater
    Princeton Showhouse
Phillip Ennis Photography

Lilac Time

This room was designed for conversation and entertaining. A set of paintings and a few knick-knacks provide some decoration without being overpowering and distracting. They are prominently and proudly displayed in a pair of recessed shelves on either side of the window. Two armchairs are set back closer to the wall to make a path so visitors can move freely around the room. The black lacquered floor is criss-crossed with lavender stripes to complement the soft color of the lavender walls. Zebra-striped pillows are an exciting, vibrant touch.

Ann Lind Bowers Interior Design and
    Decoration
2003 Women's Association of
    Morristown Memorial Hospital
    Mansion in May Showhouse
Phillip Ennis Photography

Urban Retreat

Designed as a respite from the bustle of city life, this room was to be devoid of any particular color without being dull. Textures and quiet patterns give the room a touch of ornamentation. Large windows let in lots of light that picks up the sparkle of mica-specked walls and gives the room a warm, soothing glow. Sisal apple matting carpet and various upholstery fabrics add some textural variations, ensuring that while the room was intended to be visually relaxing and calming, it is not boring. The calming atmosphere does not limit itself to the visual aspects of the room. Cozy furniture and soft textures inspire physical, visual, and mental relaxation. Off to the side, a table provides the perfect place to have a light, relaxing meal or play a quiet game of solitaire far from the frantic activity of the rest of the world.

Susan Zises Green, Inc.
2003 Kips Bay Decorator Show House
Photography by Billy Cunningham

Classic Modern Mix

A variety of different styles and influences come together in this living room. European and Asian, modern and classic, artificial and organic are all thrown into a room and mix into a very intriguing whole. Louis Seize chairs and a grand piano present an air of Western sophistication while Chinese statuary seeds the air with a hint of flavor. The chairs, the sofa, and a shelf table situated behind the sofa are all classic or imitations of classic designs. The flowing lines of the tables, woven grass rug, and rope palm pots contribute an organic element. The end result is an inviting, eclectic combination of styles and influences that make a tasteful and attractive whole.

Thomas Bartlett Interiors
2004 San Francisco Decorator
    Showcase
Matthew Millman Photography

The Great Living Room

Stately and dark colored, wood paneling presents a dignified air and gives this living room the feeling of an English country manor. Stylistically, the furniture provides modern flair, while the colors help to lighten the room. White and shades of red and green are contrast beautifully with the dark wood. The curving lines of the furniture contrast with the straight, regimented lines of the panels To add some humor, the designer included a few whimsical portraits of dogs dressed in military uniforms.

Janice Crawford, L'Interieur By J.
    Crawford, IIDA
2004 Children's Museum of Southeast-
    ern Connecticut Showhouse
Don Santos Photography

Welcoming Formality

Designer Susan Zises Green wanted to create a welcoming atmosphere in this grand and sumptuous wood paneled room. Rather than choosing a style that was stuffy and formal, she included a combination of cut velvet and cotton materials to upholster the room's furnishings, creating an inviting, "come sit down" room.

Susan Zises Green, Inc.
2003 Kips Bay Decorator Show House
Photography by Billy Cunningham

Gentleman's Library

Chris Chew designed this library as a tailored, yet casually elegant retreat from the daily demands of a hectic contemporary lifestyle. Seamlessly combining traditional English and neoclassical French with modern simplicity, the room achieves a sense of calm and balance. Tailored portieres in sheer Belgian linen soften the light that floods into the French crème painted room. At night, French guilt bronze and gunmetal sconces in the form of baroque Nubians and rococo rams heads shed light on antiqued mirror, crystal, and mirror black porcelain surfaces for a glimmering effect. A classic Knoll sofa tailored in woven herringbone linen provides contrast to the room's George III glass front bookcase and demilune consoles, both in richly colored mahogany.

Christopher Chew Interior Design & Decoration
2003 Assistance League® of Southern California Design House
Photography by Grey Crawford and Douglas Hill

Italian Palazzo Living Room

All the classic grandeur and elegance of an Italian palazzo is reproduced in this room. An elaborate marble fireplace takes center stage with acanthus leaf carvings on the mantle and a reproduction of a Renaissance painting commanding the attention of anyone who enters. Designer Joyce Hoshall chose furniture that would soften, warm, and brighten the room. Velvet upholstered chairs add luscious texture to the space, which tantalizes the senses with its classical ambiance.

Joyce Hoshall Interiors, Antiques & Collections
2003 Junior League of Sacramento Showhouse
Dave Adams Photography

Asian Inspired Living Room

The allure of the Far East is evident in James Rixner's Asian inspired living room. Softly striated walls set the tone for this serene and sophisticated environment. Vintage salon chairs from the HMS Queen Mary live comfortably with a Giacometti inspired silver leaf cocktail table and a custom designed sleek contemporary sofa. The luxurious silk fabrics used throughout give the room a gracious glow while underscoring the rich cinnabar and chartreuse palette. This unusual color combination was inspired by the rare antique Agra area rug, which anchors the seating area. The layering of periods, textures and styles creates an opulent setting with a decidedly contemporary edge, which has become Mr. Rixner's signature look.

James Rixner, Inc.
The Tomes-Higgins Showhouse
Phillip Ennis Photography

Villa Poggia: A Lifestyle for Generations

When choosing the colors for this room, designer Sarah DeWitt drew her inspiration from the Aegean Sea, the Tuscan sky, the color of young vines, and vintage wine. Blue-green plaster walls fill the room with a sense of calm. Blue wool sateen on the sofa and the celadon linen velvet on the club chair evoke the image of clear blue Tuscan skies and complement the blue-green of the walls. Looking out over the vineyards, the windows are hung with curtains made from silk the color of Catawba grapes. Over it all looms a magnificent carved stone fireplace that serves as the central focus of the room. Flanking the fireplace are a pair of immense book cabinets which house a collection of rare and antique books. The fireplace's multi-colored harlequin surround complements the colors of the rest of the room. Antique hardwood furnishings blend in with the classic elegance of the room. High ceilings add to that sense of elegance and grandeur, while comfortable furniture and warm colors create a less formal, comfortable atmosphere perfect for the intimate family gatherings the designer envisioned when creating this room.

Sarah DeWitt, DeWitt Designs
2005 Tucson Museum of Art Designer
    Showhouse
Photography by Tim Fuller

Classically Modern

A true sanctuary rich in earth tones and defined by contemporary artworks and accessories, this room is for after-dinner drinks, cigars, and conversation. Traditional furnishings anchor the space, enhanced by mohair, silk, and cashmere in monochromatic hues.

Pineapple House Interior Design®
2003 Alliance Children's Theater Guild
    Christmas House
Chris Little Photography

A Seaside Retreat

People are social beings and, for the most part, thrive in the company of others. There are times, however, when a person just needs to get away from it all, to find a quiet corner and be alone with his thoughts. This is a room for just such an occasion. Tucked away in a remote corner of the house, the room features a beautifully hand-painted floor, a comfortable leather chair, and a fabulous bar with a handsome screened wallpaper backdrop. For a truly relaxing atmosphere, the designer chose to accent the room with items reminiscent of the sea, such as the antique seashell prints, and the artistic shell mirror. Even the seaweed pattern of the wallpaper subtly evokes the calming effect of the shore.

Bonnie Battiston Interiors
2004 Children's Museum of Southeastern Connecticut Show House
Don Santos Photography

History Updated

The goal of the designer was to create a period style room that was compatible with a contemporary lifestyle. Eighteenth century architectural elements included a beamed ceiling and large fireplace common to that era. An antique china cabinet, a wooden trunk, and "country hunt" themed accessories also contribute to the period style of the room. Upholstered furniture brings in the comfort of a more contemporary period. So as to not clash with the overall décor of the room, the furniture was upholstered in a rough tweedy fabric similar to the woolen cloth in subtle browns and greens which evokes the era. Colonial and modern America have been united in a subtle and tasteful way that combines historical elegance with contemporary comfort. The room achieves a balance between past and present—keeping a foot in the present with a style that doesn't disturb the integrity of the past.

Diane Burgoyne, Allied Member ASID, IFDA, Diane Burgoyne Interiors
2002 Historical Society of Moorestown Historic Showcase House
Photography by Barry Halkin

"His" Space

Rich, warm brown tones welcome visitors into this elegant library, designed especially for the man of the house. Cherry paneling lends warmth to a room perfect for an after dinner drink or cigar. Using the rug as the basis for the room's look, designer Christian Huebner chose window treatments with wood tassel beaded trim and cherry rods and rings to complement the room's paneling. The linen covered coffee table was lacquered to give it an attention-grabbing texture. A travertine marble surround on the fireplace provides contrast to the custom cherry mantel.

Christian Huebner Interiors, Inc.
2004 Dickens House
Photography by Drew Altizer

Garden Room

A soft maize and coral color palette calms the senses in a garden room that offers a break from busy schedules. Bookcases designed by Carolyn Oliver flank one of five sets of French doors in the room and showcase a collection of whimsical, hand-painted ceramic birds. The room's abundance of light and soothing color palette provide the perfect venue for relaxation.

Carolyn E. Oliver, Oliver's – A Design
    Studio
2004 Pasadena Showcase House of Design
Mark Lohman Photography

"La Chambre de la Petite Bonne" (The Chambermaid's Room)

A red, white, and blue color palette, antique and reproduction furnishings, and authentic textiles give this room a decidedly French flair. The antique Louis XV day bed provides a relaxing place to sit or perhaps steal a few moments of sleep, and is upholstered with a red and white toile illustrating an Eighteenth century fable entitled "The Millworker, his Son, and the Donkey." A reproduction Louis XV fall front desk provides a place to write a letter. The Louis XVI style chair back was upholstered in red and white gingham to complement the day bed, while the chair seat was upholstered to match the walls, which feature a cotton lampas fabric woven to imitate a brocade.

Coffinier Ku Design, Ltd.
2001 French Designer Showhouse
Photography by Daniel Eifert

A Study in Contrasts

Designer Carole Weaks chose a color palette of reds and neutral tones, projecting an air of elegance and sophistication. Classic furnishings were chosen for both aesthetic value as well as comfort, with a glass table providing a hint of modernity. Envisioning that this study would also be used for entertaining, the closet was converted into a hidden bar, displaying a small collection of contemporary paintings to add interest and contrast to the room's classical styling.

C. Weaks Interiors, Inc.
2003 Atlanta Symphony Associates
    Decorators' Show House and
    Gardens
Photography by Delera Whitlaw
    Llewellyn

Captive Den

Shades of tan accented by sage green make a soothing, unobtrusive combination in this study. To make the most of natural light, a desk was placed in a corner between two windows, while a comfortable armchair and ottoman provide a leisurely place to sit and read. Wallpaper simulating pine panels adds to the close, comforting atmosphere of the space—a truly enjoyable place to be kept captive.

Sherry Stein, Allied Member ASID, and
    Albert Janz, IIDA, Henry Johnstone
    & Co.
2004 Pasadena Showcase House of
    Design
Photography by Alex Vertikoff

The Rooftop Suite

In the rooftop suite of the main house, the designer wanted to blur the distinction between the interior and exterior of the home. A small foyer acts as the suite's main entrance, and was covered in boxwoods to give the impression of walking through a hedge. The rooms of the suite give a baroque feel with the unexpected combinations of silks, velvets, leaves, berries, rock crystal obelisks, forged iron, bronze ornaments, and kudu horns. Intended as a space for relaxation, uninterrupted meditation, or private entertaining, this rooftop suite creates a vivid and memorable impression.

Coffinier Ku Design, Ltd.
2003 Kips Bay Decorator Show House
Photography by Mick Hales

Gem in the Rough

One of the smallest rooms in the Showhouse, principals Nina Nielsen and Sandra Harding wanted to create a little gem of a room—but not your typical polished gemstone. Using petrified woods, woods with unfinished & jagged edges, spherical & organic shapes, oxidized metals and fabrics in luxurious earth tones, the designers created a room with organic appeal. Weathered walls wrapped in lacquered rust wallpaper and iridescent pearl paint on the moldings and ceiling envelop the room in luxurious texture. Black and white framed photographs, lithographs, paintings, and furnishings give the room a contemporary flair.

Nina Nielsen & Sandra Harding, NS
    Designs
2005 The Designer Showhouse of
    New Jersey
Photography by Lydia Gould-Bessler

Expansive Solutions in Mid-Century Style

In a long, narrow room at the top of this show house, Michael Rosenberg created an artful space for retreat marked by clean styling. He divided the room into three separate sections defined by a desk area, sitting area, and a window seat for additional lounging space. A comfortable wool floor with horizontal banding adds movement and width to the room. Cream-colored armchairs keep the room floating and flowing, creating a visual unity with the floor covering. Another color would have broken up the space and distracted the eye. Color was added with chartreuse ultra suede accents that also work to add depth and movement, and maintain a fresh look. Dark walls add drama with a custom cross-hatched, hand-painted paper. Pearlized essence gives it added color and depth and adds sheen to the room. The furnishings represent a mixture of mid-century style and include a Gioponti glass table between the two cream-colored chairs, an American deco desk, 1940 Biedermeier consoles, and a reupholstered Joseph Frank stool.

Michael Rosenberg & Associates, Inc.
2002 Kips Bay Decorators' Show
    House
Photography by Peter Pierce

A Tasteful Repose

This library indulges the senses in velvety textures, vibrant colors, and stimulating patterns. Rich, chocolate brown walls provide the foundation for a tempting color palette of apple green, maize, and pumpkin. A relaxing space for renewal, where the mind and the eye are awakened.

Margaret Donaldson Interiors
2005 Charleston Symphony Orchestra
    League/ASID Designer Showhouse
Photography by Tripp Smith

Sumptuous Suite

Soft, neutral shades blanket this study in a warm, peaceful atmosphere. Inspiring tranquility, thought, and relaxation, silky textures also add luxury to the space. The suite begins with a "relaxation room"—a luxurious space with a sumptuous bed for ultimate lounging—and ends with a library/office that is every working woman's dream, if not necessity. A palette of moody bronzes spiced with raspberry sets the sensual tone, along with a rich variety of textures. Walls are lined in a tobacco-hued silky glass cloth and the floors are covered in nubby sisal. Accenting the walls are baseboard moldings of cerused oak, which repeats the cerused oak of the room's focal point, a captain's bed topped with a raspberry linen-velvet mattress cover. Texture and color are reasserted at the curved wall adjacent to the relaxation area, where custom bronze-leafed wallpaper with random swirls of raspberry jazzes up the subtlety of the previously monochromatic neutral walls.

John Barman, Inc.
2000 Traditional Home's Built for
 Women Show House
Photography by Billy Cunningham

Graceful Serenity

The designers of this room began with a design concept inspired by the rich historic architecture of the Colonial Revival home. An intriguing wall finish creates the iridescence and texture of silk. Over a sage green base paint, a champagne gold metallic glaze was applied and combed in large-scale squares that alternate between vertical and horizontal patterning. Natural elements accent the room, including exquisite silk draperies with a delicate fern motif. Custom drapery rods are made of three intertwined iron bars softly bent and twisted to look like tree branches with small iron leaves. Greenery viewed through the windows is brought inside by incorporating live plants and arrangements of natural cuttings rather than traditional bouquets. Furnishings with traditional style roots were selected because of their understated grace and simplicity. The straight lines of the French Directoire bed form a simple yet strong framework for beautiful bedding fabrics with minimal ornament. The sensual curves of both night tables and their accompanying lamps soften and balance the bed's square form. Overall, exquisite fabrics and organic themes create a sense of calm and respite—a place of natural symmetry and order.

Gail Englemann, Gail Engelmann
    Designs
Penny Lorain & Jennifer May, Lorain &
    May Design Associates
2005 Junior League of Sacramento
    Designer Showcase House
Photography by Dave Adams Photography and Lightray Photoimagery

Gingembre Boudoir

Designer Diane Boyer, ASID, created a romantic guest room appropriate to the Victorian pedigree of the home. But instead of the deep, often stuffy, Victorian colors, she selected a soft, soothing sage and ginger combination. To camouflage the cracked and pitted walls, she selected a commercial-grade wall covering with an iridescent finish. The ceiling treatment is a canvas drop cloth which was faux painted with an elaborate center medallion and texturized to complement the walls. The medallion itself echoes the turnings of the opulent canopy bed. The wallpaper border was also faux painted on canvas to match the ceiling technique.

The focal point of the room is the handsome gold-leafed metal bed lavishly dressed in silk, velvet, Egyptian cotton, and lace, enthroned on an Oriental carpet. Above the bed, like a crowning jewel, is a turn-of-the-century crystal and bronze chandelier surrounded by the hand-painted ceiling medallion. On either side of the bed, pairs of Italian reverse painted and gilded mirrors and consoles showcase candelabra lamps that are a marriage of several Old World pieces.

Diane Boyer Interiors LLC
2003 Junior League of Montclair-
    Newark Show House
Phillip Ennis Photography

Melanie's Guest Bedroom and Bath

This guest suite is defined by the use of satiny textures and gold accents. Designer Nancy Holstein used a classic approach in designing this room, which maintains a very feminine feeling. In the bathroom, a hand-painted mural gives a glimpse of the rolling hills and solitary trees of the Tuscan countryside. In contrast to the light-colored tiles and walls, the countertop is made of black concrete anchoring the room and keeping it from looking too light. The copper basin and faucet complement the colors found in the mural and maintain the historic aesthetic established in the adjacent bedroom.

Nancy K. Holstein Interiors
Children's Museum of Southeastern
    Connecticut Showhouse, 2004
Don Santos Photography

Jazz Bath

This bath suite is made up of entry, sitting room, and bathroom areas. The entire suite was designed as a tribute to Cole Porter and the 1920s with its rare wood cabinets, Art Deco walls, a marble fireplace, and luxuriously appointed rooms. The bathroom features a Jacuzzi, two showers, two commodes, and a massage table. The sitting area includes a marble fireplace and an entertainment center, and the entryway features a gallery exhibiting various 1920s themed paintings and photographs. Despite the suite being split into three different rooms, the designer made sure to include elements that would help unite the three disparate parts by using materials that extended from one area to the others. The ceramic tiles in the bathing area, for example, are continued in the sitting room as chair rail and picture moldings. Neutral colors were selected to create a backdrop for the different metals used in the furniture and black and white accents to create a proper 1920s jazzy atmosphere.

Gail Green, Green & Company, Inc.
CRI Showhouse
Phillip Ennis Photography

Enlightened From Within

Designer Jackie Naylor divided the original space into a small room with sink and commode, and a larger room featuring a vanity with mirrored walls. When the powder room was remodeled, the sink was moved into the larger room and made the focal point of the space. The new sink was made from Avonite and lit from within, shedding soft light on green and white silk panels that were placed on the wall behind it. The rest of the walls in the space feature a diamond-patterned wallcovering and small orchid photographs to fill in for live flowers. A bronze sculpture titled "Nude Female" stands in one corner and adds further drama to a stylishly elegant space.

Jackie Naylor Interiors, Inc.
2003 Atlanta Symphony Associates
    Decorators' Show House and
    Gardens
Robert Thien Photography

Clean and Classic

Rich brown walls help take away some of the chill of this powder room's white marble tiles. White molding frames the room's circular mirror and a few pieces of artwork hung on the walls, creating architectural interest. The bathtub is made from porcelain-coated steel set inside a marble surround, giving the impression that the floor had risen up and surrounded the bathtub. Like the bathtub, the shower is also covered with marble tile. The room's only window is hung with a simple window treatment that provides a homey atmosphere, while keeping with the elegance of the room's design. Simple, clean lines marry with traditional elements like the sink and molding to create a rejuvenating, grounded space.

Ashley Roi Jenkins Design
2005 San Francisco Decorator
    Showcase
Photography by David Duncan
    Livingston

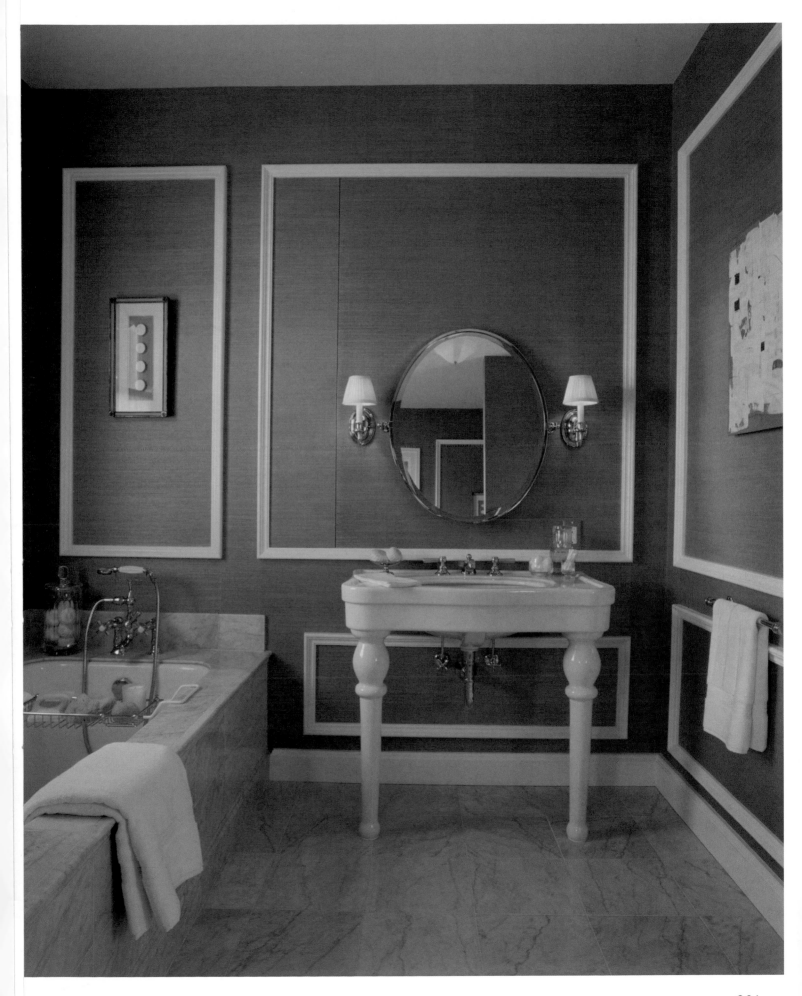

Wynwyk Green: Mrs. Cronkhite's Bath

A classic Regency patterned fabric in green and white stripes was used throughout this bath in a variety of ways in order to create harmony and visual interest. The window treatments feature the fabric hung both vertically and horizontally, as well as other classic Regency design motifs including the star and the criss-cross diamond pattern in gold and silver. These motifs, the tassels, and swags are used repeatedly throughout the room, and reflect the Regency Modern style favored by designer Gail Green. Combining classical and romantic elements, traditional and modern concepts, the style results in spaces that are spacious, airy, and uncluttered, yet rich in historical association.

Gail Green, Green & Company, Inc.
Greenwich Junior League Showhouse
Photography by Kurt Dolnier

Room Fit for a Teen

Periwinkle colored walls form the backdrop for a palette of bright colors suitable for a teenage girl. Galvanized aluminum panels create a unique message board and a place to hang posters or pictures. A bed on wheels means that the room can be rearranged according to a teenage girl's constantly changing tastes. The square pattern on the bedspread is reproduced on a larger scale on the border of the carpet. Above, the ceiling's woven pattern adds some interesting visual and textural elements. Suspended from the ceiling is a hanging desk complementing the free-flowing feel of the room. Beside the bed, small tables can be pulled close to use as bedside tables, placed around the room for decoration, or pulled together to hold drinks or snacks when friends come over. Bright colors and comfortable furniture make this a room any teenage girl would enjoy.

Kim Hrasky, Twist Interior Redesign
2004 Children's Museum of Southeastern Connecticut Showhouse
Don Santos Photography

Room for a Princess

A hand painted apple green bed surrounded by a long canopy of silk embroidered with rosebuds acts as this bedroom's focal point. The bed's curving feminine lines are mirrored in the other furnishings. Posies painted on the wall and a vintage floral chandelier reinforce the room's feminine feel. Required to work with the room's existing brown shag carpet, designer Joyce Hoshall included a lambskin rug for its texture and clarity. Adding some "big-girl glamour" to the space, a large oval mirror reflects the room's apple green and soft pink color palette. Designed with the intention of helping a young girl develop self esteem, the room does its job by making its inhabitant feel just like a little princess.

Joyce Hoshall Interiors
2003 Junior League of Sacramento
    Designer Showcase House
Dave Adams Photography

Dedicated Playroom

Here an attic was converted into a child's playroom designed to mimic a busy city. Leading up to the room, the stairway railing is in the shape of a fire hose coming from a hydrant painted on the wall, and in the background happy children cavort in the spray coming from a fire hydrant. In one corner is a fire station set in the middle of a busy city street painted on the wall. A set of bunk beds shaped like a fire engine was designed and built by world-renowned artist Red Grooms. The room was finished just after 9/11 and dedicated to America's fire men and women who lost their lives that day. Moving from the "city," in another corner is an open-air market with flower and fruit stands painted on doors leading to closets and toy storage. A set of steps lead up to an elevated nook painted to look like a city park, where the window resembles a ferris wheel, and where there is room to play a board game or have a tea party. A large room gives children plenty of room to play and have fun while colorful murals stimulate their vision and their imaginations.

Joani Stewart, Montana Avenue Interiors
2001 Assistance League® of Southern
    California Design House
Photography by Grey Crawford

Let the Spirit of Youth Soar

A small boy's love of flight inspired this room's décor. An airplane mobile glides over the bed and hot air balloons float on the bedspread and pillows. The creatively painted skylight on the ceiling and a custom designed metal magazine rack with blinking tail lights next to the bed add a fun, youthful interest to the room. Apple green walls and glazed woodwork provide a "natural" background for the room's design so that it will easily evolve with the age, interest, and needs of a growing boy.

Barbara Keenan, Keenan Interiors, LLC
2004 Charlotte Symphony Guild ASID
   Showhouse
Photography by Sean Busher

A Child's Playroom

Here is a place for young children to let their imaginations soar while surrounded by colorful and stylish furnishings. A child's creativity is inspired in a room void of televisions and computer games! This is a space that immerses children in complex design ideas to encourage them to see the world in a new, fresh way, and rocket to great ideas.

The inspiration for this room came from the Andy Warhol prints of his "Endangered Species" series painted in 1983. A custom built loft occupies one corner of the playroom. Scarves hang from the bottom to make a little nook underneath the loft. In the opposite corner from the loft a drawing table made entirely of Corian sits between two windows to make the most of natural light while children color and draw. Soft fabrics and rounded edges make the room comfortable and safe for running around. The spatter-painted wallpaper gives the room a sense of whimsy while the bright colors add to the energy of this dynamic playroom.

Leslie Driscoll, ASID, Driscoll Design
2004 Children's Museum of Southeastern Connecticut Showhouse
Don Santos Photography

A Day at the Fair

This room was created while a mother was expecting her fourth child, "Roman." The designers' goal was to welcome the baby boy in a playful and warm manner using a whimsical "Day at the Fair" fabric. The design reflects a fresh approach to a nursery, yet the elements have a timeless appeal. It is a comfortable, cozy and soothing place for Roman and a nurturing place for midnight feedings. The glider and ottoman are upholstered in celery gingham with beige piping which is repeated in the crib linens. The tent canopy over the crib is a design element repeated in the tent display shelf and again on the ceiling. The stripes coming out from the chandelier are subtle enough to suggest the inside of a tent. It was important that the entire family be welcomed here, so a window seat large enough for several people and a child's table and chair set for Roman's older siblings were added. The handpainted crib and toybox depict characters found in the vintage Fair pattern and are on the stepstool as well. While a welcome place for the family to gather, this room is nostalgic and subtle, yet fun and fresh.

Roselle McConnell, Infant Interiors and
    Ramona O'Donnell, Ramona
    Designs
2004 Newport Designer Showhouse
Olson Photographic

Colonnade Entry

This walkway/colonnade acts as the entry to a magnificent house, and features an Old World Venetian motif throughout. Solid Moorish gold stone flooring was laid in an irregular geometric pattern and interspersed with large medallions with a faded colored pattern reflecting ancient days of Italy. Tiles in a similar pattern were used to border the walkway and risers on the stairs leading to the gorgeous gardens in front of the house. Indoor/outdoor canvas in a cool, soft sage green was hung from the arches and tied back with a big knot of the same fabric to coordinate with the cushions on the area's iron seating. Plaster beams painted to resemble aged wood were stenciled in a Venetian motif with colors to imitate those in the floor medallions and to reflect the architecture of the home. The beams' distressed and worn finish gives the impression of original designs recently uncovered from years of paint and weather. At the end of the colonnade and near the entrance to the home, a beautifully carved antique mirror hangs above an antique iron console with a stone top, reflecting the length of the colonnade. On the other side of the doorway is an antique Italian ceramic cherub holding up foliage and greenery. Evoking a feeling of cool, casual elegance, relaxation, and ancient beauty, this space is an introduction of what the interior of the house has to offer.

Joani Stewart, Montana Avenue
    Interiors
2002 Pasadena Showcase House of
    Design
Photography by Douglas Hill

Moonlight Terrace

The aroma on this terrace is sweet and succulent. Iceberg roses and night blooming jasmine climb the white lattice trellis and cover the walls with white and green foliage. Elegant iron furnishings with a nickel finish are not your typical outdoor patio lounge chairs. Indoor/outdoor upholstery used for the furnishings does not have to be removed in inclement weather, while the fill on the cushions is also mold and water resistant, so it can stay outside and won't fade or deteriorate for years to come. The covers on the lounges and chairs have skirts to the floor and tassels on the corners to create a sophisticated, formal atmosphere. The candelabrum in the center of the table is a refurbished antique chandelier furnished with candles instead of electric lights, providing a romantic glow during intimate nighttime meals.

Joani Stewart, Montana Avenue
    Interiors
2003 Pasadena Showcase House of
    Design
Photography by Douglas Hill

Glamour in the Great Outdoors

Inspired by future plans to add a pool and water features to the home, designer Annette Hannon designed this space with entertaining in mind. Three separate areas are defined by the use of outdoor rugs, which are soft on the feet and easy to clean. A commercial grade teak cabana provides an elegant setting for dinner parties, while a secluded area outside the living room allows guests to escape the crowd and engage in quiet conversation. The area close to the built-in grill works as an extension of the family room, with plush seating, an edited bronze coffee table, shaped topiaries, and a three-panel screen to conceal outdoor necessities. Hannon chose a warm color to balance the coolness of the home's gray exterior. Exchanging chocolate brown railings for the existing white ones helped to ground the space and establish a more graceful transition between landscape and architecture. This space demonstrates that outdoor living can be just as intimate, glamorous, and versatile as indoor life.

Annette Hannon Interior Design, Ltd.
2005 National Symphony Orchestra
    Decorators' Show House
Photography by Angie Seckinger

Moroccan Dining Patio

The enjoyment of outdoor dining is combined with the exotic atmosphere of a Moroccan courtyard on this patio. Terra cotta colored chairs and couches line both sides of the patio and complement the patio's floor tiles. Embroidered pillows and potted palms add some exotic flavor. The walls of the patio and the dining area are covered with tadelakt, a lime colored plaster wall coating found in many traditional Moroccan homes. Colorful Moroccan patterned tiles cover the floor of the dining area, complemented by blue-cushioned chairs with yellow accent pillows.

Dolores Kroop, Padua & DK Designs
2002 Pasadena Showcase House of
    Design
Photography by Jenifer Godwin-Minto

The Italian Loggia

Glorious architecture and natural light direct the mix of texture and detail in this all-season space. A custom designed mosaic floor features an international mix of materials such as slate, marble, limestone, and travertine, which echo the color of the home's exterior. Taking inspiration from a historic Italian motif, a custom mural was painted on the ceiling to complement the existing murals found on the ceilings of adjacent rooms. Custom damask print window treatments, Italian furnishings, and an artist's digital reproduction of historic butterfly specimen boxes complete the look of the loggia, which seamlessly blends the home's interior and exterior spaces.

Carolyn E. Oliver, Oliver's – A Design Studio
2002 Assistance League® of Southern California Design House
Peter Christiansen Valli Photographic Services

Art Moderne Solarium

Taking inspiration from the existing pattern in the leaded glass window transom, designers Sabrina Balsky and Peter Mason replaced linoleum flooring with stunning sky blue marble comer inserts and black granite with chunk mother of pearl individually laid into the grout lines. Next, the room's dated oak ply walls were painted a cool ice blue, the color echoed in the custom made 12' leather sofa. The primary wall of the room was covered in hand painted and aged mirrored panels by artist Brent MacDougall. A French 1940s chandelier in the shape of a crystal ship was added for a touch of whimsy. Acting as a multifunctional space, this Art Moderne inspired solarium provides a sunny interior with cool style suitable for breakfast, luncheons, intimate candlelit dinners, and quiet solitude.

Sabrina Balsky & Peter Mason, Sabrina
   Balsky Interior Design, Inc.
2005 The Designer Showhouse of
   New Jersey
Photography by Lydia Gould Bessler

Youthful Sunroom

A combination of Sunbrella® and Crypton fabrics were used for ease of maintenance and durability. A loose-laid woven vinyl tile was also chosen for its low-maintenance quality. Designer Emily Walser decided that the original sleeping porch would best function as an informal family room and overflow sleeping space for teenagers. Fresh colors and a modern aesthetic retain a youthful energy and create a space perfect for young ladies and gentlemen, but are also sophisticated enough for an older crowd.

Emily B. Walser, ASID, From Start to
    Finish Interiors
2005 The Women's Club of Raleigh
    ASID Showhouse
Dustin Peck Photography

239

Opulent Tropical

Designer Camille Saum transformed a brick-faced addition into an opulent solarium filled with classical elegance and a touch of whimsy. Undulating chaise lounges in a shiny lime green vinyl are juxtaposed against traditional furnishings and accents, and provide contrast to natural materials like sea grass floor coverings, bamboo lamp, and tortoise shell doors. A color palette of lime, tangerine, tortoise shell, cinnamon, and honey is realized in the room's irregular vertical stripes and loose lattice designs. Overall, an elegant mix of lively colors, rich textures, and rustic luxury creates a wonderful transitional room that bridges the home's interior and outdoor living environments.

Camille Saum Interior Design, LLC
2004 National Symphony Orchestra
    Decorators' Show House
Photography by Gordon Beall

Outside, In

This solarium's tromp l'oeil ceiling gives the impression of standing under the protection of a decorative iron gazebo. Rattan furnishings, sea grass rug, and organic inspired prints maintain the fresh feeling of the outdoors, which is enhanced by the sound of a trickling wall-mounted fountain.

Margaret Donaldson Interiors
2002 Charleston Symphony Orchestra
    League Designer's Showhouse
Photography ©Leslie Wright Dow

Mid-Century Style, In a Country Manor

Irwin Weiner took a unique approach in designing this sunny addition of a traditional Bucks County, Pennsylvania, old stone manor house. French macramé chairs from the 1960s and other mid-century furnishings from the designer's own collection are juxtaposed with an 18th century Dutch Colonial armoire and other, more traditional style antiques. Mid-century paintings above the sofa punctuate the room with bright colors, adding geometry. Sunny yellow draperies in an Osborne and Little fabric add some formality to the space, which is elegant but casual—a perfect mix for this window-lined addition.

Irwin Weiner Interiors, Ltd.
2005 Village Improvement Association
    of Doylestown, Pennsylvania,
    Designer House & Gardens
Photography by Bruce Buck

Rooftop Retreat

Here the designers' goal was to transform the outdated terrace of this Pacific Heights house into a modern retreat, making the most of the terrace's view of the San Francisco Bay and the Marin Headlands. On the west side of the terrace, slate was laid down to create a stone patio, where two lounge chairs take advantage of the sunlight. Furniture and materials were selected to resist wind and rain and weather gracefully over time. Vertical-grain red cedar boards were laid in such a way as to draw attention to the view of the Golden Gate Bridge. The nautical style railing was painted to emulate the color of the bridge and maintains the clean, modern aesthetic established by the terrace's furnishings.

Laura White & Jude Hellewell, Outer
     space Landscape Architecture
2004 San Francisco Decorator
     Showcase
Photography by Jude Hellewell

Designers

Linda Allen Designs
Los Angeles, CA
(323) 466-4800
www.lindaallendesigns.com

Arbogast Design Group
Carmichael, CA
(916) 481-6267
www.arbogastdesign.com

Sabrina Balsky Interior Design, Inc.
New York, NY & Toronto, Canada
(212) 585-0441 & (416) 486-7898

John Barman, Inc.
New York, NY
(212) 838-9443
www.johnbarman.com

Thomas Bartlett Interiors
Napa, CA
(707) 259-1234
www.thomasbartlettinteriors.com

Bonnie Battiston Interiors
Stonington, CT
(860) 535-3136

Beret Design Group, Inc.
Upper Montclair, NJ
(973) 857-4714
www.beretdesigngroup.com

Ann Lind Bowers Interior Design
    and Decoration
Far Hills, NJ
(908) 234-1334

Diane Boyer Interiors LLC
Verona, NJ
(973) 857-5900
www.dianeboyerinteriors.com

Diane Burgoyne Interiors
Moorestown, NJ
(856) 234-9660
www.dianeburgoyneinteriors.com

Caldwell-Beebe, Ltd.
McLean, VA
(703) 790-1183
www.caldwell-beebe.com

Christopher Chew Interior Design
    & Decoration
Los Angeles, CA
(323) 304-2281

Coffinier Ku Design, Ltd.
New York, NY

(212) 715-9699
www.coffinierku.com

Robert Couturier, Inc.
New York, NY
(212) 463-7294
www.robertcouturier.com

Crème Fresh For the Home
Woodland Hills, CA
(818) 883-1030
www.cremefresh.net

DJS Interiors
Mt Laurel, NJ
(856) 222-0304

C. Davis Interior Design
Kennesaw, GA
(770) 443-6545
www.cdavisinteriordesign.com

DeWitt Designs
Tuscon, AZ & Sioux Falls, SD
(520) 622-1326 & (605) 335-4354
www.dewittdesignsinc.com

Margaret Donaldson Interiors
Charleston, SC
(843) 722-2640
www.margaretdonaldsoninteriors.com

Leslie Driscoll, ASID, Driscoll Design
North Stonington, CT
(860) 535-1680

Gail Engelmann Designs
Woodland, CA
(530) 908-9404

From Start to Finish Interiors
Raleigh, NC
(919) 782-5542
www.fstfinteriors.com

Gail Green, Green & Company, Inc.
New York, NY
(212) 737-4804
www.greenandcompanydesign.com

Susan Zises Green, Inc.
New York, NY
(212) 824-1170
www.susanzisesgreen.com

Susan Gulick Interiors
Reston, VA
(703) 674-0332
www.susangulickinteriors.com

Annette Hannon Interior Design, Ltd.
Burke, VA
(703) 978-1487
www.annettehannon.com

Harmonious Living by Tish Mills
    Design Group, LLC
Atlanta, GA
(404) 281-8889
www.harmoniousliving.net

Nancy K. Holstein Interiors
Mystic, CT
(860) 245-0004

Joyce Hoshall Interiors, Antiques,
    & Collections
Folsom, CA
(916) 765-7538

Howarth Designs LLC
Arlington, VA
(703) 671-8448
www.howarthdesigns.com

Christian Huebner Interiors, Inc.
San Mateo, CA
(650) 558-8700
www.huebnerinteriors.com

Infant Interiors and Ramona Designs
Newport, RI
(401) 842-0010
www.infantinteriors.com

Inspired Spaces Kitchen and Bath Design
Waterford, CT
(860) 447-8927
www.inspiredspaceskb.com

Interior Impressions, Inc.
Bethesda, MD
(301) 657-4490
www.intimp.com

Interiors by Mimi, Inc.
Mount Holly, NC
(704) 820-9136
www.interiorsbymimi.com

Jon Jahr & Associates, Inc.
Newport Beach & Beverly Hills, CA
(949) 646-6098 & (310) 300-4021
www.jonjahr.com

Ashley Roi Jenkins Design
San Francisco, CA
(415) 409-1689
www.arjdesign.com

Susie Johnson Interior Design, Inc.
Austin, TX
(512) 328-9642
www.susiejohnson.com

Henry Johnstone & Co.
Pasadena, CA
(626) 395-9575
www.henryjohnstoneco.com

Keenan Interiors, LLC
Charlotte, NC
www.keenaninteriors.com

L'Interieur By J. Crawford, IIDA
Westerly, RI
(401) 348-0045
www.linterieur-jcrawford.com

Deborah Leamann Interiors
Pennington, NJ
(609) 737-3330
www.deborahleamanninterior.com

Gail Lieberman
Baltimore, MD
(443) 415-4418

Victor Liberatore Interior Design
Baltimore, MD & Boca Raton, FL
(410) 444-6942 & (866) 474-0036
www.victorliberatoreinteriordesign.com

Lorain & May Design Associates
Sacramento, CA
(916) 481-0660
www.lorainandmaydesign.com

Lori Graham Lindsay Hair Interiors
Washington, DC
(888) 336-4192
www.lglhi.com

MV Design Group
Burbank, CA
(818) 557-3346
www.mvdesigngroup.com

McIntosh Interiors
Atlanta, GA
(404) 588-1951
www.mcintoshinteriors.com

Montana Ave Interiors
Santa Monica, CA
(310) 260-1960
www.montanaaveinteriors.com

Robin Muto
Positive Environments Interior
   Design Studio
Rochester, NY
(585) 232-6030

NS Designs, LLC
New York, NY
(212) 722-5225
www.nsdesigns.net

Jackie Naylor Interiors, Inc.
Atlanta, GA
(404) 814-1973

Karina Oldemans Interior Design
Los Angeles, CA
(310) 820-0320
www.karinaoldemans.com

Oliver's: A Design Studio
Pasadena, CA
(626) 449-3463
www.oliversinteriors.com

Outer space Landscape Architecture
San Francisco, CA
(415) 643-1840
www.outerspacela.com

Padua & DK Designs
San Marino, CA
(626) 796-0629

Pineapple House Interior Design®
Atlanta, GA
(404) 897-5551
www.pineapplehouse.com

Point One Architects + Planners
Old Saybrook, CT
(860) 395-1354
www.pointonearchitects.com

Shane Reilly Inc.
New York, NY & San Francisco, CA
(415) 602-4454
www.shanereilly.com

The Replogle House Interiors
Mechanicsburg, PA
(717) 691-1185
www.reploglehouseinteriors.com

James Rixner, Inc.
New York, NY
(212) 206-7439
http://jamesrixner.com

Michael Rosenberg & Associates, Inc.
New York, NY
(212) 757-7272
www.mrosenbergassociates.com

St. Charles of New York
New York, NY
(212) 838-2812
www.stcharlesofnewyork.com

Camille Saum Interior Design, LLC
Bethesda, MD
(301) 657-9817
www.camillesaum.com

Joy Sawyer
Wickford, RI
(401) 295-9900

Marjory Segal
The Well-Furnished Garden & Home
Bethesda, MD
(301) 469-6979

Matthew Patrick Smyth, Inc.
New York, NY
(212) 333-5353
www.matthewsmyth.com

Tkid, inc.
San Francisco, CA
(415) 522-2443
www.tk-id.com

Twist Interior Redesign
Marion, MA
(508) 317-2889
www.twistinteriorredesign.com

Suzanne Tyler Design & Chinese Red
Stonington, CT
(860) 535-3605

Nancy Van Natta Associates
San Rafael, CA
(415) 456-3078
www.van-natta.com

Pauline Vastardis Interiors
Moorestown, NJ
(856) 866-1625
www.pvinteriors.com

Clive Christian Washington
Washington, DC
(202) 314-5700
www.clive.com

C. Weaks Interiors, Inc.
Atlanta, GA
(404) 233-6040

Irwin Weiner Interiors, Ltd.
New York, NY
(212) 308-2235
www.irwinweiner.com

Douglas Weiss Interiors
Atlanta, GA
(404) 875-5544
www.douglasweiss.com

Cheryl Womack Interiors
Atlanta, GA
(404) 256-0704

Show House Events

ALLIANCE CHILDREN'S THEATER GUILD'S CHRISTMAS HOUSE
Atlanta, GA
(404) 733-4620
www.alliancechristmashouse.org
www.alliancetheatre.org

The Alliance Theatre is one of the country's few major regional theatres that produces professionally staged work for children with the same high production values as its adult offerings. Its eleven production season on two stages is complemented by extensive and innovative education and community outreach programs. For over 30 years, Christmas House has continually helped subsidize theatre tickets to the Alliance Children's Theatre productions for thousands of Georgia students and economically disadvantaged youth annually. Patrons to Christmas House tour a beautiful home showcasing the talents of some of Atlanta's finest designers, shop for extraordinary gifts and unique decorations in the boutique, and lunch on site at Café Noel.

ASSISTANCE LEAGUE® OF SOUTHERN CALIFORNIA DESIGN HOUSE
Hollywood, CA
(323) 469-1973
www.designhousela.org

Assistance League® of Southern California is a nonprofit organization established in 1919 that provides a broad range of essential human services and economic development activities to low- and moderate-income residents within Hollywood, the San Fernando Valley, and the greater Los Angeles area through a partnership of dedicated volunteers and staff.

ATLANTA SYMPHONY ASSOCIATES DECORATORS' SHOW HOUSE AND GARDENS
Atlanta, GA
(404) 733-4935
www.decoratorsshowhouse.org

The Atlanta Symphony Associates (ASA) is the volunteer organization for the Atlanta Symphony Orchestra. Membership is open to both men and women volunteers interested in supporting the Orchestra. Members may belong to any of the seven membership units. For over fifty years, the Associates have been the backbone of the ASO with its varied fund-raising, community outreach and educational efforts.

AUSTIN SYMPHONY DESIGNER SHOWHOUSE
Austin, TX
(512) 637-0329
www.symphonyshowhouse.org

The Women's Symphony League of Austin is an organization of volunteers who provide service and financial support for the Austin Symphony Orchestra for their educational programs as well as opportunities for children and the community to develop a deeper appreciation of music. Over the past eighteen years, the WSL has contributed more than 3.2 million dollars to the Austin Symphony Orchestra, and members give over 10,000 volunteer hours yearly to educational and fundraising projects.

CASHIERS HISTORICAL SOCIETY DESIGNER SHOWHOUSE
Cashiers, NC
(828) 743-7710
www.cashiershistoricalsociety.org

CHARLESTON SYMPHONY ORCHESTRA LEAGUE/ASID DESIGNER SHOWHOUSE
Charleston, SC
(843) 723-0020
www.csolinc.org

CSOL, Inc. is a not-for-profit organization of music lovers committed to keeping the music playing in Charleston and the Lowcountry by supporting the Charleston Symphony Orchestra through education, scholarships, audience development, and fundraising events.

CHARLOTTE SYMPHONY GUILD ASID SHOWHOUSE
Charlotte, NC
(704) 972-2003
www.symphonyguildcharlotte.org

The Symphony Guild of Charlotte, formerly the Charlotte Symphony Women's Association, was created in 1950 to support the Charlotte Symphony Orchestra and symphonic music in the Charlotte area. Through the group's fundraisers, it has given more than $4 million to the Charlotte Symphony Orchestra. This tremendous support has been possible only through the efforts of volunteers and the generous support of the community.

CHILDREN'S MUSEUM OF SOUTHEASTERN CONNECTICUT SHOWHOUSE
Niantic, CT
(860) 691-1111
http://childrensmuseumsect.org

The Children's Museum of Southeastern Connecticut is designed to enhance learning for children through grade 5 and the adults in their life. The Museum encourages a hands-on interactive approach to play that is designed to stimulate curiosity and imagination. A combination of real objects from the museum's collections as well as reproduced objects, thematic play, and challenging "games" are used to empower children to explore, ask questions, and have fun.

DEBORAH HOSPITAL FOUNDATION DESIGNERS' SHOW HOUSE
Brown Mills, NJ
(609) 893-3372
www.deborahfoundation.org

Deborah Heart and Lung Center, located in Burlington County, Browns Mills, NJ, is the only specialty center in the region focused exclusively on heart, lung and vascular disease, and the only freestanding medical institution in New Jersey licensed to perform open-heart surgery on adults and children. The Deborah Hospital Foundation is a grass-root volunteer and chapter network that consists of 25,000 volunteers located along the Eastern seaboard from Maine to Florida. Established in 1974, the Foundation is composed of 130 community-based chapters and acts as the fundraising arm of the hospital.

THE DESIGNER SHOWHOUSE OF NEW JERSEY
Englewood Cliffs, NJ
(201) 503-0470
www.designershowhousenj.com

EUREKA SCHOOLS FOUNDATION HOME SHOW
Granite Bay, CA
(916) 791-4939
www.eurekaschoolsfoundation.org

The Eureka Schools Foundation (ESF) boasts a $1.9 million, 12-year-old commitment to parent-driven support of enrichment programs throughout the Eureka Union School District. This commitment began with the initial vision and support by the Pioneer 100 members and their generous donations. Each year, more than 4000 students from eight schools enjoy ESF-generated dollars earmarked for music, science, art, computers, foreign language, athletics, and library programs.

THE HAMPTON DESIGNER SHOWHOUSE
Southampton, NY
(631) 745-0004
www.hamptondesignershowhouse.com

JUNIOR LEAGUE OF GREATER PRINCETON SHOWHOUSE
Trenton, NJ
(609) 771-0525
www.jlgp.org

The Junior League of Greater Princeton is an organization of women committed to promoting voluntarism, developing the potential of women, and improving communities through the effective action and leadership of trained volunteers. Its purpose is exclusively educational and charitable.

JUNIOR LEAGUE OF MONTCLAIR-NEWARK SHOW HOUSE
Montclair, NJ
(973) 746-2499
www.jlmn.org

JUNIOR LEAGUE OF SACRAMENTO DESIGNER SHOWCASE HOUSE
Sacramento, CA
(916) 437-1649
www.jlsac.org

The Junior League of Sacramento, Inc. is an organization of women committed to promoting voluntarism, developing the potential of women, improving communities through the effective action and leadership of trained volunteers, and enhancing the well-being and future of Sacramento's children through the dedicated action of volunteers. The organization develops trained leaders; designs, administers and sometimes originates innovative community programs; assesses and builds public awareness of critical community needs; contributes valuable and significant volunteer hours toward the improvement of the community; and raises money for the community through funded projects, direct grants, and endowments.

KIPS BAY DECORATOR SHOW HOUSE
New York, NY
(212) 755-5733
www.kipsbay.org/showhouse.html

Kips Bay Boys & Girls Club has been focused on enhancing the lives of New York City's children. Kips Bay provides essential after-school and enrichment programs for over 12,000 young people between the ages of 6 and 18, at nine locations in the Bronx borough of New York. Today, the Club is proudly one of the most prominent and responsive youth development agencies in New York City and the "flagship" of the Boys & Girls Clubs of America.

LOURDES HEALTH SYSTEM SHOW HOUSE
Camden, NJ
www.lourdesmed.org/showhouse

MARIN DESIGNERS SHOWCASE
Marin County, CA
(415) 479-5691 or (415) 479-5710
www.centerforleadershipmarin.org

This annual fundraising event, presented by the Auxiliary of the Centre for Volunteer and Nonprofit Leadership of Marin (Center), has been a Marin tradition since 1969. Though the Center is the main beneficiary, the Auxiliary also donates a percentage of the Showcase proceeds to one or several Marin nonprofits through the Heart Tug Program. The Center seeks to enrich and strengthen volunteerism and nonprofit organizations in its mission to develop a vital and engaged community dedicated to building and sustaining quality of life.

NATIONAL SYMPHONY ORCHESTRA DECORATORS' SHOW HOUSE
Washington, D.C.
(202) 416-8150
www.kennedy-center.org

Formed in 1941 as a committee of the NSOA, the Women's Committee for the National Symphony Orchestra has a membership of approximately 1,000 in six geographic chapters. The Women's Committee endowment provides funding for the Principal Oboe Chair, the sixth NSO subscription week, one NSO guest conductor week annually, and one NSO Young People's Concert annually. The Show House is held each October, and is one of the oldest and most successful in the nation. In the past 28 years, the show house has raised over 6.3 million dollars for the NSO.

NEWPORT DESIGNER SHOWHOUSE
Newport, RI
(401) 846-5574
www.newportshowhouse.org

Pasadena Showcase House for the Arts
San Marino, CA
(626) 578-8500
www.pasadenashowcase.org

The Pasadena Showcase House for the Arts ("PSHA") is a non-profit California corporation. The Pasadena Showcase House of Design ("Showcase") is produced as the annual benefit, combining the efforts of PSHA members with over 50 designers who transform the interior and grounds of an estate selected by PSHA. The success of Showcase has resulted in cumulative donations almost $14 million to the Los Angeles Philharmonic, schools, and other local non-profit organizations. PSHA programs funded from Showcase proceeds include the Music Mobile™ Program, the Pasadena Showcase House Youth Concert for children, and the Pasadena Showcase House Instrumental Competition for young musicians.

Rochester Philharmonic Orchestra Symphony Showhouse
Rochester, NY
(585) 454-7311
www.rposhowhouse.org

The Rochester Philharmonic Orchestra's biennial Symphony Showhouse is the organization's signature fundraiser for its educational programs. The RPO has shown an unsurpassed dedication for providing educational programs for all ages, particularly to the area's youth. Each Showhouse is planned by a volunteer committee. A steering committee of twenty leads eighty other volunteers in various sub-committees. In addition to private and self-guided tours, the 2004 Symphony Showhouse featured music salons with RPO musicians, afternoon teas, culinary showcases and a murder mystery dinner.

San Francisco Decorator Showcase
San Francisco, CA
(415) 447-3117
www.decoratorshowcase.org

Since 1977, the annual San Francisco Decorator Showcase has benefited San Francisco University High School's Financial Aid Program. Thanks to the generosity of the patrons and the participation of designers, students, parents, faculty trustees, alumni, friends and visitors to the Showcase, this event allows SFUHS to offer financial aid to nearly 20% of its students. Since 1977, more than $8 million has been raised in tuition assistance.

Tucson Museum of Art Designer Showhouse
Tucson, AZ
520-624-2333
www.tucsomnuseumofart.org

The Designer Showhouse is a biennial event organized by the Tucson Museum of Art League as a fundraiser for the Tucson Museum of Art. Very popular with the community, Designer Showhouse has given many deserving designers the exposure they need to gain new clients while supporting one of the oldest arts organizations in the state. The Tucson Museum of Art League is a group of diverse individuals whose mission is to support the Tucson Museum of Art through fundraising events.

The Women's Club of Raleigh ASID Showhouse
Raleigh, NC
(919) 782-5599
www.womansclubofraleigh.org